THE Feminist ACTIVITY BOOK

The Feminist Activity Book
Copyright © 2016 Gemma Correll

ISBN 978-1580056304

Library of Congress Cataloging-in-Publication Data is pending.

Published by
Seal Press
An imprint of Perseus Books
A Hachette Book Group company
1700 Fourth Street
Berkeley, California
sealpress.com

Cover and Interior Illustrations and Design by Gemma Correll
Print Production by Tabitha Lahr
Printed in the United States of America

LSC-C
10 9 8 7 6

THE Feminist ACTIVITY BOOK

GEMMA CORRELL

SEAL PRESS

A FEMINIST ABC

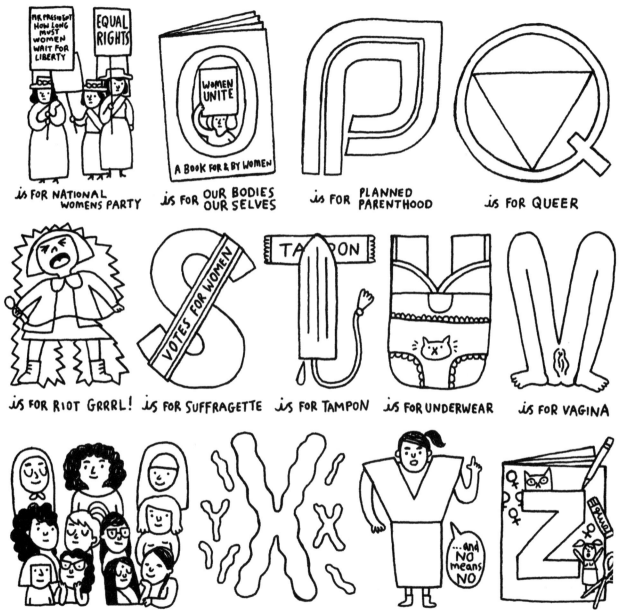

is FOR NATIONAL WOMENS PARTY

is FOR OUR BODIES OUR SELVES

is FOR PLANNED PARENTHOOD

is FOR QUEER

is FOR RIOT GRRRL!

is FOR SUFFRAGETTE

is FOR TAMPON

is FOR UNDERWEAR

is FOR VAGINA

is FOR WOMYN

is FOR CHROMOSOMES

is FOR YES MEANS YES

is FOR ZINES

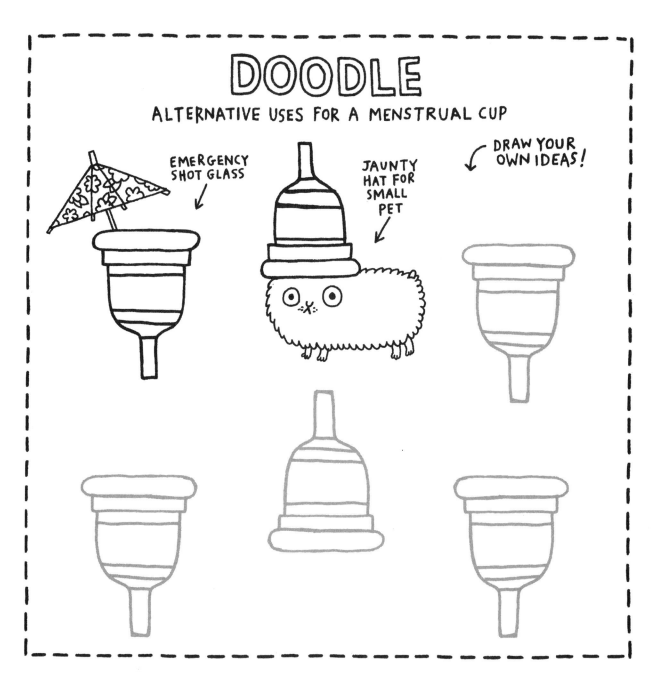

WORK OUT IF
YOUR FAVORITE
MOVIES PASS THE
BECHDEL TEST.

TITLE _____
DOES IT PASS? Y☐ N☐

TITLE _____
DOES IT PASS? Y☐ N☐

TITLE _____
DOES IT PASS? Y☐ N☐

TITLE _____
DOES IT PASS? Y☐ N☐

TITLE _____
DOES IT PASS? Y☐ N☐

TITLE _____
DOES IT PASS? Y☐ N☐

TITLE _____
DOES IT PASS? Y☐ N☐

TITLE _____
DOES IT PASS? Y☐ N☐

DOODLE

DESIGN SOME AWESOME (IF IMPRACTICAL...) CONDOMS!

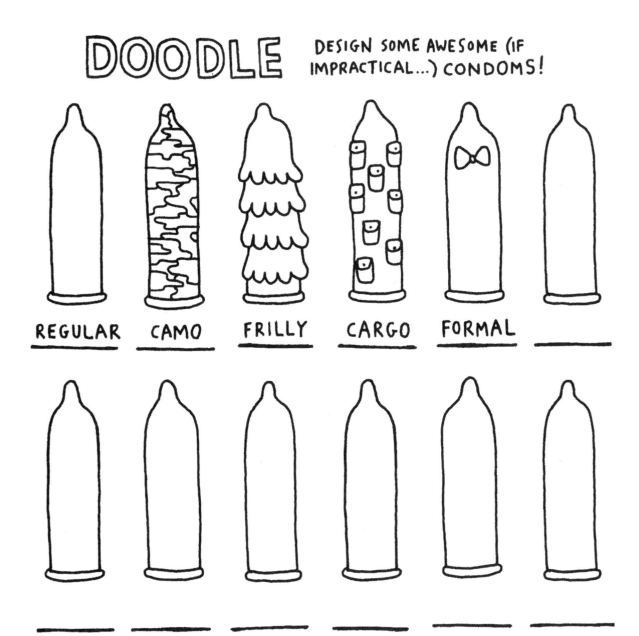

REGULAR CAMO FRILLY CARGO FORMAL

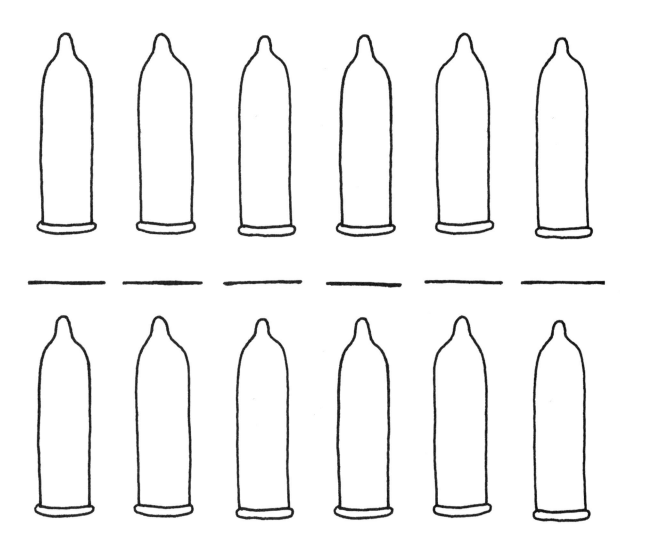

NOTES _____

NOTES _____

NOTES _____

NOTES _____

NOTES _____

NOTES _____

NOTES ⎯⎯⎯⎯⎯

NOTES ⎯⎯⎯⎯⎯

NOTES ⎯⎯⎯⎯⎯

NOTES ⎯⎯⎯⎯⎯

NOTES ⎯⎯⎯⎯⎯

NOTES ⎯⎯⎯⎯⎯

NOTES _____

NOTES _____

NOTES _____

NOTES _____

NOTES _____

NOTES _____

MATCH THE GENDER IDENTITY WITH THE CORRECT DEFINITION

Cis

Trans

Gender Fluid

Agender

Intersex

Demi

GENDER IDENTITY DOES NOT ALIGN WITH THE GENDER ASSIGNED AT BIRTH

BORN WITH REPRODUCTIVE ORGANS, CHROMOSOMES OR ANATOMY THAT DO NOT FIT THE TYPICAL DEFINITION OF MALE OR FEMALE

FEELS A PARTIAL CONNECTION TO A GENDER IDENTITY

GENDER IDENTITY ALIGNS WITH THE GENDER ASSIGNED AT BIRTH

GENDER IDENTITY IS NOT CONFINED TO ONE GENDER CATEGORY

DOES NOT IDENTIFY AS ANY GENDER (AKA-GENDER NEUTRAL)

WHERE'S WENDY?

THERE ARE 500 CEOS AT THIS FORTUNE 500 PARTY.
CAN YOU FIND 26 WOMEN, 4 AFRICAN AMERICANS AND 15 ASIAN / LATIN AMERICANS?

KEY — WHITE MALE   AFRICAN AMERICAN*   FEMALE   ASIAN / LATIN AMERICAN

* YEP, JUST 5.2% OF FORTUNE 500 CEOS ARE WOMEN. AND LESS THAN 1% ARE AFRICAN AMERICAN.** ONLY 3% ARE ASIAN AMERICAN OR LATIN AMERICAN.

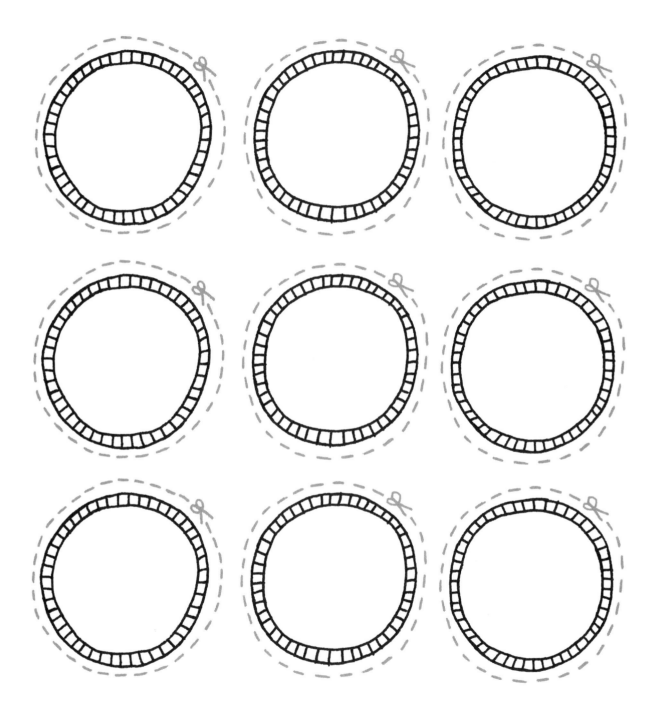

DOODLE
FEMINIS-T-SHIRTS

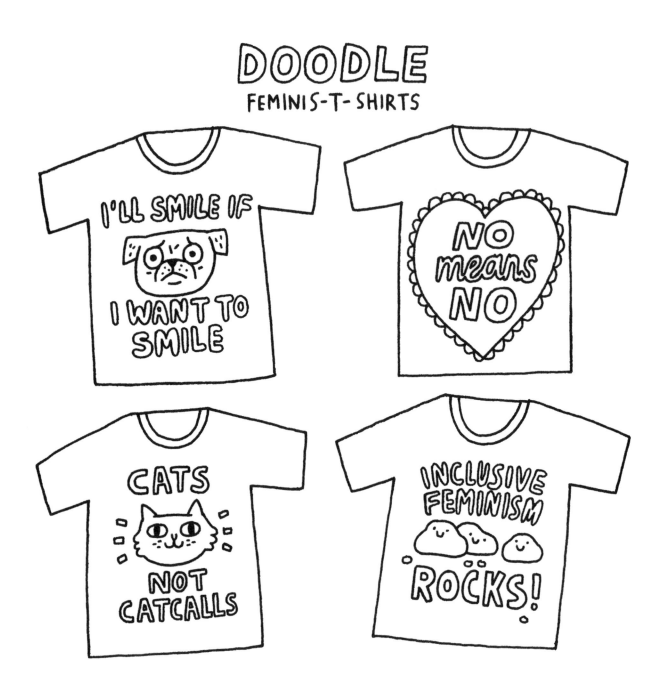

I'LL SMILE IF I WANT TO SMILE

NO means NO

CATS NOT CATCALLS

INCLUSIVE FEMINISM ROCKS!

WORD  FIND

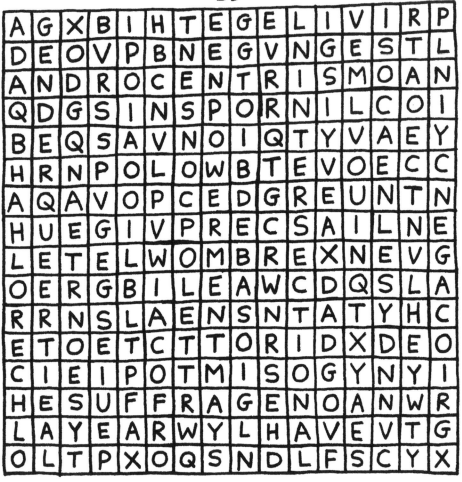

A	G	X	B	I	H	T	E	G	E	L	I	V	I	R	P
D	E	O	V	P	B	N	E	G	V	N	G	E	S	T	L
A	N	D	R	O	C	E	N	T	R	I	S	M	O	A	N
Q	D	G	S	I	N	S	P	O	R	N	I	L	C	O	I
B	E	Q	S	A	V	N	O	I	Q	T	Y	V	A	E	Y
H	R	N	P	O	L	O	W	B	T	E	V	O	E	C	C
A	Q	A	V	O	P	C	E	D	G	R	E	U	N	T	N
H	U	E	G	I	V	P	R	E	C	S	A	I	L	N	E
L	E	T	E	L	W	O	M	B	R	E	X	N	E	V	G
O	E	R	G	B	I	L	E	A	W	C	D	Q	S	L	A
R	R	N	S	L	A	E	N	S	N	T	A	T	Y	H	C
E	T	O	E	T	C	T	T	O	R	I	D	X	D	E	O
C	I	E	I	P	O	T	M	I	S	O	G	Y	N	Y	I
H	E	S	U	F	F	R	A	G	E	N	O	A	N	W	R
L	A	Y	E	A	R	W	Y	L	H	A	V	E	V	T	G
O	L	T	P	X	O	Q	S	N	D	L	F	S	C	Y	X

CAN YOU FIND... ANDROCENTRISM, INTERSECTIONAL, GENDER, SEX, QUEER, MISOGYNY, ENPOWERMENT, HERSTORY, SUFFRAGE, VULVA, VAGINA, BRA, CONSENT, WOMB, AGENCY, PRIVILEGE, CIS, TRANS?

(WORDS GO HORIZONTALLY, VERTICALLY, DIAGONALLY, BACKWARDS AND FORWARDS)

DOODLE

WHAT WOULD YOUR FEMINIST UTOPIA LOOK LIKE? DRAW IT HERE!

CAN YOU HELP RASHIDA FIND HER WAY TO WORK WITHOUT ENCOUNTERING ANY PATRIARCHAL BULLSHIT?

HERE ARE SOME <u>MALE</u> NIPPLES.

CUT THEM OUT AND STICK THEM OVER PICTURES OF UNSIGHTLY <u>FEMALE</u> NIPPLES TO MAKE THEM ACCEPTABLE TO BE SEEN IN PUBLIC OR ON SOCIAL MEDIA!

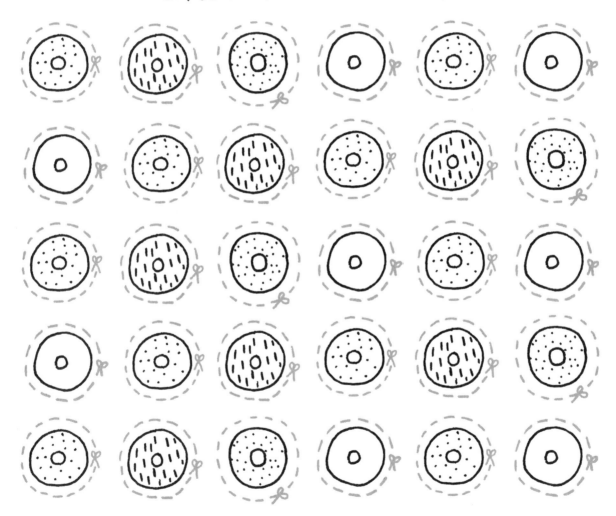

DESTROY THE PAGE-TRIARCHY!

DOES THE PATRIARCHY MAKE YOU ANGRY?
TAKE IT OUT ON THIS PAGE! RIP IT UP! SCRIBBLE ALL OVER IT!
SMASH IT WITH A HAMMER! IT'LL BE CATHARTIC.

RIDDLES

Mr Brown is giving his class apples as a reward for doing their work. (Mr Brown is a little strange)

If Dave gets 100 apples for doing his work,
and Daniella gets 77 apples for doing her work,
and Denise, who is African-American, gets 68 apples,
and Daya, who is Hispanic, gets 58 apples,
and Doris, who is disabled, gets 22 apples,

Is that fair?

A: No, it bloody well isn't.
But replace apples with cents and you have the breakdown of the wage differences in the USA.
It's currently estimated that it will take 118 years for the gender wage gap to close.

Elena says that she's not a FEMINIST because, although she believes in equality, she doesn't hate boys, and she likes wearing make-up and pretty dresses...

Q: So, what SHOULD Elena call herself?

A: Elena can still call herself a FEMINIST.
Feminism is NOT man hating, or anti-feminine.

SOCIAL MEDIA BINGO

WRITE SOMETHING ABOUT FEMINISM ON SOCIAL MEDIA. MARK THE SQUARE WHEN YOU SEE THE COMMENT. PLAY ALONE OR WITH FRIENDS! SO MUCH FUN!

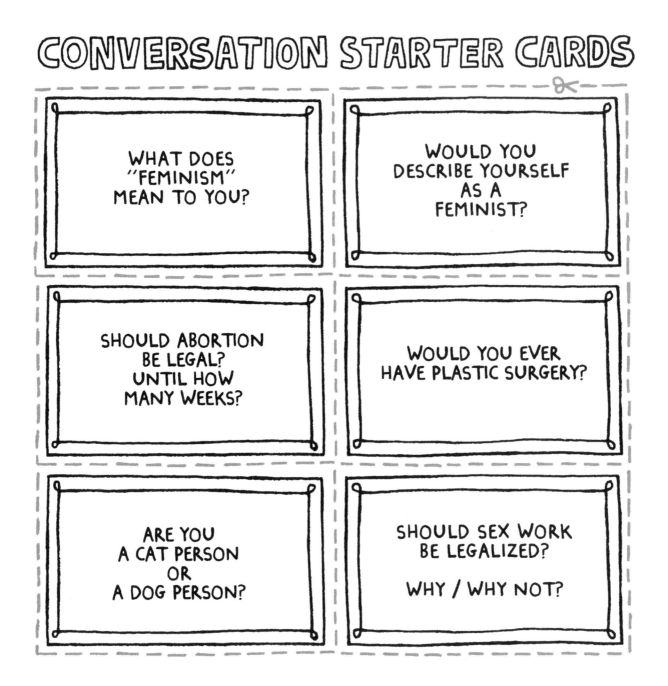

START A CONVERSATION ABOUT FEMINISM, SOCIAL ISSUES OR SNACK FOODS
WITH YOUR FRIENDS OR FAMILY OR CAT WITH THESE HANDY CARDS ...

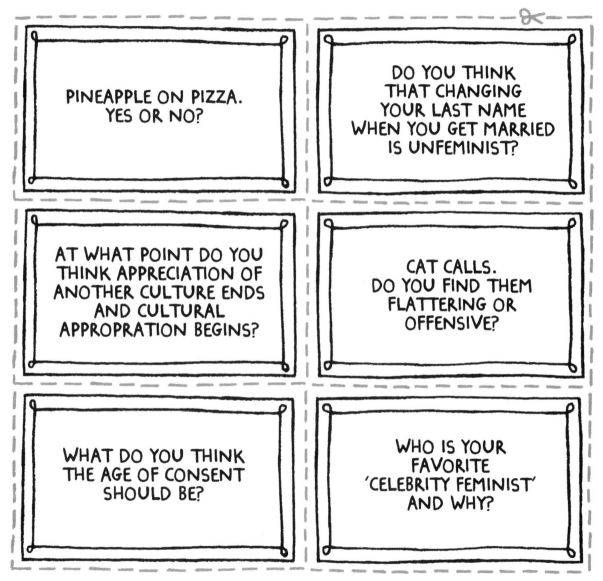

CRAFTY CORNER

MAKE YOUR OWN GENDER PRONOUN BADGE TO LET PEOPLE KNOW WHICH PRONOUN YOU USE FOR YOURSELF.

IF YOU'RE NOT SURE WHAT PRONOUNS A PERSON USES, JUST ASK THEM (POLITELY!)

ASK ME ABOUT MY PRONOUNS

JUST MY NAME PLEASE

SOME PEOPLE PREFER NOT TO USE PRONOUNS AT ALL.

HE
HIM/HIS/HE

SHE
HER/HERS/SHE

THEY
THEM/THEIRS/THEMSELF

ZE
ZE/ZIR/ZIRSELF

XE
XEM/XYR/XYRS/XEMSELF

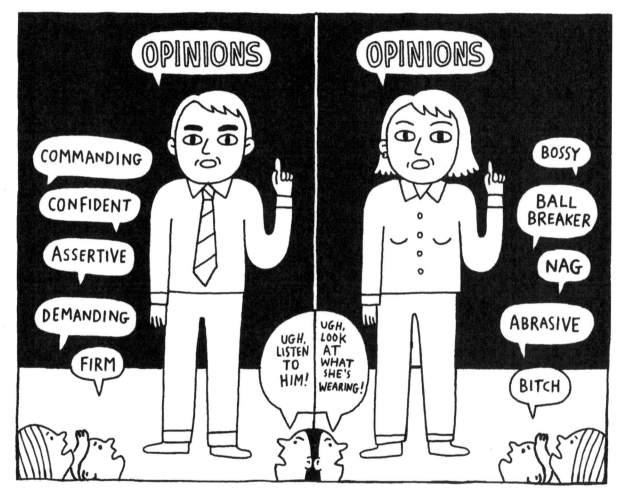

SOLUTION : WHILE MEN ARE APPLAUDED FOR ASSERTIVENESS, WOMEN ARE MALIGNED AND CALLED NAMES. AN ARGUMENT BETWEEN MEN IS A 'HEATED DISCUSSION', BUT WHEN IT'S BETWEEN WOMEN IT IS A 'CATFIGHT'.

CAN YOU SPOT SIX THINGS THAT ARE WRONG WITH THIS PICTURE?

SOLUTION – 1. THE S IN 'TOY SHOP' IS BACKWARDS. 2. 'GIRLS' IS SPELLED INCORRECTLY. 3. THE BIRD HAS THREE LEGS. 4. THE KID ON THE LEFT HAS HIS HAT ON UPSIDE DOWN. 5. THE TOYS ARE ARRANGED IN A WAY WHICH REINFORCES UNHELPFUL SOCIETAL GENDER STEREOTYPES BY ASSUMING THAT BOYS ONLY WANT TO PLAY WITH 'TOUGH', OR 'CLEVER', TOYS AND GIRLS ARE ONLY INTERESTED IN PLAYING WITH TOYS THAT ARE 'PRETTY', OR DOMESTIC. 6. CATS CAN'T TALK, SILLY!

FEMINIST VALENTINES TO CUT OUT & COLOR

THE SEXUAL HEALTH CROSSWORD

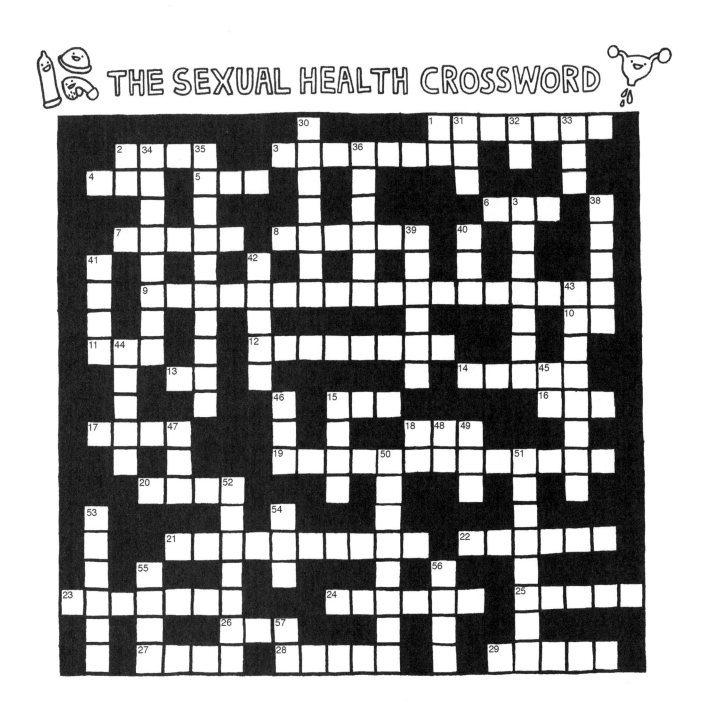

CLUES

ACROSS

1. ANIMALS THAT HUMP A LOT, APPARENTLY
2. THE   — SLANG TERM FOR GONORRHEA
3. WASHING OR CLEANING OUT THE VAGINA
4. INFECTION OF THE BLADDER OR KIDNEYS
5. WHERE THE CONTRACEPTIVE IMPLANT IS INSERTED
6. VIRUS THAT CAUSES GENITAL WARTS (ACRONYM)
7. TYPE OF GOWN YOU MIGHT WEAR AT THE DOCTOR'S
8. STI MARKED BY GENITAL PAIN AND SORES
9. FULL NAME OF THE I.U.D
10. TURNED   — FEELING SEXUALLY AROUSED
11. THE CATHOLIC CHURCH REGARDS ABORTION AS ONE
12. HORMONE THAT THE MINI-PILL DOES NOT CONTAIN
13. "... MEANS (46 DOWN)"
14. THE HEAD OF THE PENIS
15. BRITISH WORD FOR BUTTOCKS
16. DRUGS THAT ARE NON-PRESCRIPTION (ACRONYM)
17. BRITISH SLANG WORD FOR SEXUAL INTERCOURSE
18. A CHILD OR YOUNG PERSON
19. ANOTHER NAME FOR CONDOMS
20. A DOCTOR THAT SPECIALIZES IN WOMEN'S REPRODUCTIVE HEALTH (ABBR)
21. TO TOUCH OR RUB ONESELF IN A SEXUAL MANNER
22.   PHASE — THE SECOND HALF OF THE MENSTRUAL CYCLE, AFTER OVULATION
23.   SYNDROME, AKA. SYMPATHETIC PREGNANCY
24. THE NARROW OUTER END OF THE UTERUS
25. SLANG TERM FOR (56 DOWN)
26. A SMALL PROTUBERANCE, SUCH AS THE CLITORIS
27. TO BREED (USUALLY REFERRING TO ANIMALS)
28. THE EXTERNAL PARTS OF THE FEMALE GENITAL ORGANS
29. FLUID RELEASED FROM THE PENIS DURING ORGASM

DOWN

1. A TYPE OF HEALTH WORKER (ABBR)
2. A TYPE OF CROSS-SECTIONAL X-RAY
18. A BRAND OF LUBRICANT
30. PERMISSION FOR SOMETHING (e.g. SEX) TO HAPPEN
31. THE   OF (30 DOWN)
32.   SEXUAL — ATTRACTED TO BOTH MEN AND WOMEN
33. SLANG TERM FOR A BREAST
34. TUBAL   — SEVERING AND TYING THE FALLOPIAN TUBES — PERMANENT BIRTH CONTROL
35. PLANNED   — PROVIDER OF REPRODUCTIVE HEALTH SERVICES IN THE US AND INTERNATIONALLY
36. MATERIAL THAT THE NON-HORMONAL I.U.D IS USUALLY MADE FROM
37. DEPO   — THE CONTRACEPTIVE INJECTION
38. MEMBRANE THAT SURROUNDS OR PARTLY COVERS THE VAGINAL OPENING
39. MARGARET   — BIRTH CONTROL ACTIVIST, EDUCATOR, WRITER AND NURSE
40. A TRADITIONAL PLACE TO HAVE SEX
41. TO TOUCH WITH THE LIPS
42. MATERIAL THAT MOST CONDOMS ARE MADE FROM
43. THE   ACT — PASSED IN 1873 PROHIBITING THE "TRADE OR CIRCULATION OF OBSCENE LITERATURE" (i.e. LITERATURE RELATED TO BIRTH CONTROL)
44. HOW A YEAST INFECTION FEELS
45. "(13 ACROSS) MEANS   !"
46. THE CERVICAL   — A FORM OF BARRIER CONTRACEPTION
47. HOMOSEXUAL
48. U.S. STATE (ABBR) WHERE (31 DOWN) IS 17
49. DENTAL   — PROTECTS AGAINST STIS DURING ORAL SEX
50. A ONCE-COMMON MEDICAL DIAGNOSIS FOR WOMEN WHO WERE SAID TO BE "SEXUALLY FRUSTRATED"
51. THE MALE SEX GLANDS
52. OFFENSIVE, OR IMMORAL, ACCORDING TO SOCIETY
53. VOLUNTEER THAT HELPS PATIENTS GET TO THE DOOR OF A CLINIC e.g. (35 DOWN) SAFELY
54. A SLANG WORD FOR (29 DOWN)
55. THE FEMALE REPRODUCTIVE CELL
56. PUBIC   — TINY INSECTS THAT INFEST PUBIC HAIR
57. BACTERIAL OVERGROWTH IN THE VAGINA (ACRONYM)

✿ A GLOSSARY OF TERMS ✿

ANDROCENTRISM - - emphasizing MASCULINE interests and focusing on the MASCULINE point of view.

BODY POSITIVITY - the ACCEPTANCE of one's OWN BODY, whatever its SIZE or SHAPE and the acceptance of OTHER PEOPLE's bodies.

CONSENT — PERMISSION for something (e.g. SEX) to happen.

GENDER BINARY - the DIVISION of the World into things that are "for MEN" (MASCULINE) or "for WOMEN" (FEMININE)

HERSTORY — History considered or presented from a FEMINIST view-point, or with SPECIAL ATTENTION to the experience of WOMEN.

HETERONORMATIVITY — the belief that HETEROSEXUALITY is the ONLY "normal" OR "natural" EXPRESSION of SEXUALITY.

INTERSECTIONALITY — the belief that EVERYONE - not only White, able-bodied, cisgender* women - should be included in FEMINISM.

*NOT SURE WHAT "CISGENDER" MEANS? GO TO THE SOLUTIONS PAGE

MANSPLAINING — When a man explains something to a WOMAN that she OBVIOUSLY already knows.

MISOGYNY — a strong DISLIKE or HATRED of WOMEN.

PATRIARCHY - a system of Society or government in which MASCULINITY is valued more than FEMININITY, AND men hold the POWER and WOMEN are largely EXCLUDED from it.

PRIVILEGE - the IDEA that we ALL have advantages over other people, e.g. being able-bodied, male, white or educated.

RAPE CULTURE - the NORMALIZATION of SEXUAL ASSAULT in a society.

SOLUTIONS

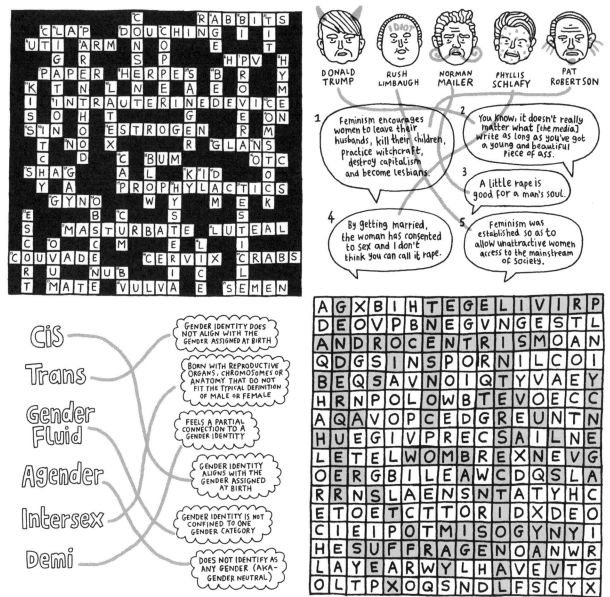

Acknowledgments

Thank you to Stephanie Knapp and everybody at Seal Press for their indispensible help and support. Thanks Tori Cann, Siofra Connor and Amber Green, three fantastic feminist friends (say that ten times fast!) from back home in Naaarwich who inspired me to make this book fun and accessible to a wide range of people, as well as providing ideas, tea and cake. And to the rest of my friends and family from the UK and the US (and beyond!) for your continued support—and, as always, thank you Anthony for bringing me green tea in the morning and helping with all the scanning, and Mr. Pickles and Bella for cuddles when I needed them the most.

Selected Titles from Seal Press

Screw Everyone: Sleeping My Way to Monogamy, by Ophira Eisenberg. $16, 978-1580054393. From her first kiss to saying "I do," *Screw Everyone* is an honest, hilarious chronicle of how one woman discovered herself, conquered her fears, and even found the "real thing"—one promiscuous encounter at a time.

Full Frontal Feminism: A Young Woman's Guide to Why Feminism Matters, by Jessica Valenti. $17, 978-1580055611. *Full Frontal Feminism* is a smart and relatable guide to the issues that matter to today's young women. This edition includes a new foreword by Valenti, reflecting upon what's happened in the seven years since *Full Frontal Feminism* was originally published.

Things No One Will Tell Fat Girls: A Handbook For Unapolagetic Living, by Jes Baker. $16, 978-1-58005-5826. Featuring notable guest authors, *Things No One Will Tell Fat Girls* is an invitation for all women to reject fat prejudice, learn to love their bodies, and join the most progressive, and life-changing revolution there is: the movement to change the world by loving their bodies.

Hes a Stud, She's a Slut, and 49 Other Double Standards Every Woman Should Know, by Jessica Valenti. $15, 978-1580052450. Whether With sass, humor, and in-your-face facts, this book calls out the double standards that affect every women and give them the tools to combat sexism and hypocrisy.

Gender Outlaws: The Next Generation, by Kate Bornstein and S. Bear Bergman. $16.95, 978-1580053082. Together with writer, raconteur, and theater artist S. Bear Bergman, Bornstein collects and contextualizes the work of this generation's trans and genderqueer forward thinkers.

A Little F'ed Up, by Julie Zeilinger. $16, 978-1580053716. In this accessible handbook, Zeilinger takes a critical, honest, and humorous look at where young feminists are as a generation, and where they're going—and she does so from the perspective of someone who's in the trenches right alongside her readers.